HÔTEL DE LA PROVIDENCE

poems by

Maya Ribault

Finishing Line Press
Georgetown, Kentucky

HÔTEL
DE LA PROVIDENCE

Copyright © 2020 by Author Maya Ribault
ISBN 978-1-64662-181-1 First Edition
All rights reserved under International and Pan-American Copyright Conventions. No part of this book may be reproduced in any manner whatsoever without written permission from the publisher, except in the case of brief quotations embodied in critical articles and reviews.

ACKNOWLEDGMENTS

With much gratitude to the editors of the following publications where these poems, sometimes in different form, first appeared:

Bloodroot (forthcoming): "A Breton Wife" and "A Breton Ghazal"
Cloudbank: "Dolphins" and "Horses"
North American Review: "Alegría"
The New Yorker: "Bees"
The New Yorker: "Society of Fireflies"
The Southampton Review Online: "A Channel Swim"

My abiding love and gratitude to Muchi, Sarah, Mick, Elo, and Oli and all my family on both sides of the Atlantic, living and long gone; to my friends, far, near, and dear; to my fellow poets, writers, and artists of all stripes—with special thanks for the invaluable poem feedback provided; to my students and readers, past and future; to my mentors and teachers through the years—with special thanks to Megan Mayhew Bergman, April Bernard, Sven Birkerts, Henri Cole, Annie Finch, Barry Goldensohn, Kathleen Graber, Edward Hirsch, Major Jackson, Keetje Kuipers, and Mark Wunderlich for guiding these poems and this poet along the way; and for Brittany, a country unto itself.

Publisher: Leah Maines
Editor: Christen Kincaid
Cover Art: Barbara Heim
Author Photo: Jessica Licklider
Cover Design: Elizabeth Maines McCleavy

Printed in the USA on acid-free paper.
Order online: www.finishinglinepress.com
also available on amazon.com

Author inquiries and mail orders:
Finishing Line Press
P. O. Box 1626
Georgetown, Kentucky 40324
U. S. A.

Table of Contents

My Urban Monastery 1

Dolphins 2

The Cicada 3

I Will Paint Your Nails 5

A Breton Wife 6

A Breton Ghazal 8

A Channel Swim 9

Haphazard Prayer 10

The Sailboat 12

This Plane 14

Café du Monde 15

Feminine Mystique 17

Blood, Rain 18

Alegría 19

Cordelianella 20

Constellations, Discarded 21

The Valley 22

Bees 23

A Larchmont Elegy 24

Cathedral Café 25

The Trouble Sometimes with Losing a Sock 26

Armpits 27

Dream Distortions 28

Dear Jigsaw 30

Horses 31

Society of Fireflies 32

For Mémé, Grand-Père, Nanny, and Koey

Marie-Thérèse Nogues Ribault (1914–2017)
Jean-Baptiste Ribault (1908–1976)
Anne Hutchins Rivinus (1916–2010)
Francis Markoe Rivinus (1915–2006)

With abiding love and affection

MY URBAN MONASTERY

After his nature walk, a man stops for a cigarette
break by a footbridge; the shrubs sprout, sport greener
blankets than even yesterday. Oh, to inhabit
the earth like a dog on a trail. What's in an hour?
A citified log stretched across a creek sniffs a sewer.

While one apartment museums collector plates,
another amasses grandfather clocks. How we live
on in cramped spaces like boxed ants. Our small fates
snow down like cherry blossoms in the wind and have
infiltrated the playground at dusk finding no grave.

While I yearn for the faraway beaches of Brittany—
their tides, their amethyst veins, their shrimp and mollusk
puddles—my friend seeks solace again in Capri.
Older now than Mozart and Jane Austen, we ask
of art what it wills through us, to fill silence like a monk.

DOLPHINS

Broccoli-crêpe evenings top pizza parlor
picnics while this-and-that knickknack stores
sell "Finding Nemo" towels, seashells polished
by machines, and t-shirts that won't stop
screaming; arcade games team up with fry-filled
cones. This boardwalk thirsts for solitude.
In either direction, a beach, not home, extends
for miles. Past a cluster of bronze men flirting,
past houses bored by ocean views, past
a Labradoodle circle-family, I walk to that edge
where summer gives way to dunes, where a pod
of dolphins alights on sunstruck waves as if
placed there for my delight alone, so near me
I slip into their slick-smooth skins. In the city
again, I spill out my story too soon to convent
ears and lose that strange sensation of morphing
into the animal who still burns in my cells.

THE CICADA

In the June-soaked tree of a Provençal hostel
a cicada lived free. She sang and she danced,
bike-wind whipping through her Rapunzel hair.

In her red espadrilles, she roamed rosemary hills,
bought tart blushing cherries from a mountainside,
ate thyme-soaked olives by a lake, basking

in an opera by Verdi. Days, weeks, she spent
in the lavender fields, filling soft notebooks
with arias at once insignificant and clear,

like the brook in the village, the stones
of the square. Night scattered her Sirocco dreams
down Milky Way paths. When the Mistral

swept in with his careless bite, at French-uncle
speed, she fled to a monastery high up in the hills.
An abbess ant in lay clothes with a tidy white bun

answered the front door. "You may come in,
demoiselle. You may stay for as long as you please,
but we do not dance here, and we do not sing.

We work hard and we pray every day." The cicada,
ashamed, stared down at her feet, her espadrilles
tattered and torn at the toes. But soon she discovered

her convent groove: she enjoyed peeling carrots
in silence and eating the daily chocolate bread snack,
though at mass she only pretended to kneel.

"This will not do," boomed the abbess with a gaze
that pierced through. "All this wanderlust
in your blood! Can't you see you are lost?"

On a night without a moon and without even one star,
our cicada escaped though she doesn't know how.
Her espadrilles guided her to the nearest train station.

How the words rang and rang as she caught the next train,
and the next, and the next: Off to Salzburg, Copenhagen.
On to Venice! O Ancient Alchemy! Come back to me.

Breathe in my blast of colors, my decaying opulence.
Linger sipping a cappuccino on the tawdry side of town.
Forever lost, gallivant about my labyrinthine alleyways.

I WILL PAINT YOUR NAILS

The-Sun-Never-Sets for the canaries
found dead in August cages; Maliblue-
Lagoon for the bedroom door you shut;
Tuxedo-Beau for the seaweed patches
the tide cloaks, then reveals; Coconut-
Waltz for my cat's belly and yesterday's
tango; Rose-Against-Time for the blood
accrued on sheets; Lime-Slime for the faded
ottoman I keep but never chose; Clementine-
Fine for the confidences of my forties; Bare-
My-Soul for I-don't-want-you-to-see
therapy; Lavendurable for the Sénanque
pilgrimage I walk for you; Linger-Over-
Coffee for the earth where I bury you; Pearl-
Swirl for the ever-sheltering Breton sky.

A BRETON WIFE

While you pretended to be a pirate
or a soldier and collected tadpoles in jars,
I played *marelle* and threaded daisies into crowns.
I wore my hair in two thick tresses down my back.
Remember when *le maître* caught you speaking Breton
and punished you to fifty courtyard laps
with that silly cowbell tied round your neck?
So we both grew up in Treguier,
I with my seamstress grandmother,
you with your nine sisters and brothers.

At sixteen, at the close of the St. Yves pardon,
your stocky silhouette burned a quiet
shape into the cathedral's altar.
For almost a year, I feigned not knowing you.
When you stopped by with daffodils,
I hid in the outhouse until you left.

Off you sailed to Newfoundland,
like your father and grandfather,
on your first cod-fishing expedition.
Each Sunday I allowed myself one mark
in the back of my missal.
Thirty-three penciled sticks accumulated there
while I passed my brevet exam,
picked blackberries for jam,
and sewed a dress for the new doctor's wife.

By Christmas we were married.
Little Annick held my train down the aisle
and all the way to our wedding feast.
At first I missed Grandmother like rain
after too many days of sunshine,
even though we visited her often for a *pot-au-feu*.
But I knew I was a lucky wife.
You didn't take to cider like other Breton men.
Instead you savored your paper with a pipe
and the clickety-clack of my needles
knitting a small blanket by the fire.

This year you sailed out before the daffodils could bloom.
Our last morning together, you asked me to refill
your bowl until the coffee carafe was empty.
The lilacs have since come and gone
and the frogs croak painfully into the night.
Soon the ferns will invade our side path to the river
and I will have gathered mushrooms in the woods
more times than I care to recall.
When Annick and I walked past those two
entwined pines today, how I envied them!
Grandmother says the baby will arrive before you do.

A BRETON GHAZAL
Pour Anatole Le Braz (1859–1926)

Tonight the Ankou, a draped skeleton with a scythe, rimes in a hurry.
Unless ready for his cart, steer clear of him amid the pines of Brittany.

Some possess the gift of sight; they can reach beyond what's visible.
                                                                Anatole
and his friends pointed them out with dread in the once-upon times
                                                          of Brittany.

Have you ever glimpsed the Bag-Noz, the phantom boat, floating,
                                                              roaming
the waters around Ile de Sein, avoiding the rugged shorelines of
                                                          Brittany?

For one gold ring, Mona trespassed upon a sandy tomb, bit off a finger.
Puss ravaged her pretty face. She used to sew hemlines in Brittany.

Someone was nearing death: the carpenters never mistook the boards'
rattle in the attic at night, anticipating the next coffin of Brittany.

The shady parish girl birthed seven babies who all disappeared.
Spot her now near the Calvary, suckling her seven little swine in
                                                         Brittany.

The melodic bells you sometimes hear far off the coast in the distance—
how can you resurrect what's left of Ys? The lost chimes of Brittany.

Maïa, what returns to you now, so far from your homeland? An
                                                        afternoon
at Trestrignel; sand, rocks, and sea; the taste of nectarines in Brittany.

A CHANNEL SWIM

At high tide in April, we caught the sun's sleeve
after school in our underwear—how the water
chilled our brains into a mushy orchard, numbing
our toes and fingers purple-yellow like Mardi-Gras
confetti. I clutched our mother's neck but then
so did my brother. That's why we weren't allowed
to watch *Jaws*. You shouldn't watch it either.
The seaweed rocks below were Raggedy Ann
monsters waiting to pull us under. I sought out
turquoise patches as if lapis lazuli treasures
anchored by sand, transfixed by prodigal rays.
Instead of Jacques Prévert, Grand-Père showed up
for our picnic decked out in his three-piece suit,
with his hat and cane. Tomatoes and hard-boiled
eggs make for great sea food: first bite, then dip
to salt. I never enter water again without
returning to our English channel, although
it's all chlorinated now. Who will let me in
to the pool after the gardens close? I'll even
admit to liking the safety of lanes, and my fellow
lappers—that one's a Phish show without the pot,
this one's a mad-dash afternoon cat. Still, at dusk
it grips me, that cod-fisherman's fear: each crossing,
a treacherous routine, salting our scales silver.

HAPHAZARD PRAYER

In 1889 Jean-Baptiste prayed for courage, sailing
from St. Malo to Newfoundland at fourteen.
To the necessity of movement, he bowed—
thirty-tree trips in a lifetime of cod-fishing.

A turn-of-the-century chambermaid, for forty years
Marie-Joseph endured endless days of menial tasks
to send her daughter to a Parisian boarding school.
For her, everything required silent determination.

Across the Atlantic, Gertrude turned to literature
and travel after becoming deaf at twenty-one.
With only silence to guide her in her eighties,
she flew to India to study with Maharishi.

In the Pacific, Koey witnessed the unimaginable;
in that vast ocean, he misplaced all his tears.
He returned from World War II a changed man.
Hear him now whistling up a Wissahickon trail.

In Le Havre bomb shelters, Marie-Thérèse breastfed
my father. When she miscarried, a nun blamed her.
We Skype now across binding time, space—her idea.
As a schoolgirl, she dreamed of England, Canada.

In the 1920s, Boston bullies tied shy Anne to a track
while all her hopes wept, all her dreams woke.
Because of her sex, her parents never offered college.
Stubborn, Anne lived and planned, cared and acted.

While all my hopes wake, all my dreams sleep, I trudge
through rows of post-it tasks (my independence).
Remembering my ancestors, I try to live, plan, care, act.
At forty-one (to my surprise), I no longer wish for a child.

But how I ache for more time, for Brittany, for poetry.
Sometimes I even pray haphazardly for courage:
I summon a house by the sea, walls of honeysuckle.
Stop? I will not, but I cannot keep on moving.

THE SAILBOAT

Like a shelled almond squeezed
between an unruly thumb and a salty forefinger,
I pop. Don't just
harness the wind, outpace him.

You used to need me
for cod-fishing, for exploring further, farther,
for bloody battles and imperial conquests,
for unnamable trades too. Don't

blame me you who created me
out of your necessity,
who can dispense with me now, the way you
dispensed with horses, reserving them
for your leisure, or your gambling habit. I am
only a tool, like a knife or a phone.
I'll try not to

mention those sunset clichés,
those star-and-moon bonanzas. But permit me
a few shimmerings—
a dragonfly, some water sparkles. It is not

a return to being needed
I seek, those high moments of shame
and glory, the days of shipwrecks,
rats and scurvy. It is not mastery either;
the man who rented me today navigates
like a boy. You watch me

from the bridge, you've
always liked the sight of white sails
in the distance. What is it about
me that spells escape
for you? Don't think

I don't recognize a wind-eye,
a no-sail-zone. This too can
be living.

THIS PLANE

stokes its power, hides its hand
longer than necessary before launching
down the runway at breakneck speed
into a takeoff that always astounds me.

I watch the clouds accommodate forests,
a shadow skim a swamp (it's a blotch
moving across a landscape). Side by side
mansions gloat. In a cove of parallel docks,
sailboats at rest mimic toothpicks.

The Mississippi weaves along
as highways do, finds its way to the Gulf,
or trails off. The river itself has a will, desires
to change course, divert from Baton Rouge,
chart another path entirely. But the engineers
naysay: the ports are set, set, set.

During the descent to New Orleans,
the plane's shifting cross defines itself further,
even manages form, and I start to feel
the relief of wings, my childish delight
at spotting turquoise shapes below.

CAFÉ DU MONDE
For Louis Moreau Gottschalk (1829-1869)

Louis, let us meet there on a late autumn day,
after you return from Rio. I'll order us
beignets to share, two mugs of café au lait.

We'll sit among the tourists, you
in a smart dandy's suit, your moustache curling
into a smile, me dressed in my newfound self.

Dissipate my fears, Louis, with your "Ojos
Criollos," your "Bamboula," your "Night
in the Tropics." Like me, you possessed

the soul of an exile before ever touring
Europe, the Caribbean, and the Americas,
and you too found your art in the cracks

of continents, in the swirl of cultures
colliding, contrary winds out of which
you wrested your own songs.

How you then fit into the web of everything
pulling me siren-like towards New Orleans
with its pecans on the ground, its afternoon duos,

its shrimp Po' Boys, and even, even
its kitschy Bourbon Street. O Crescent City,
balm to my Southern wound. O Café du Monde.

Balconies will toss out moss bouquets
to honor our obscurest follies. Come one,
come all, let's gather up the night and dance,

drum out the beat of centuries in the square.
Sorrow? We'll invite her in. She's a mother's voice
calling us by our forgotten name. A lullaby

eclipses a crescendo. A wistful note,
like a last harbor wave, slips into a grand finale.
The pianist hurries through the slow movement.

Linger there longer, I say to him,
the way heat makes one sluggish,
more capable of siestas and awakenings.

FEMININE MYSTIQUE

I thought about God, of her shyness,
how she'd like us to know she's not a jerk.
And could we sometimes take note
of her good ideas? For example, llamas
and fallopian tubes. For her holiday party,
she bakes lemon meringue, rhubarb, cherry,
and pecan pies. She enjoys organizing
her button collection by color. In the spring,
she treats herself to bouquets: daffodils
in March, tulips in April, peonies in May.
Occasionally she hides under another
kid's blanket for comfort. On Sunday:
church choir, then lunch out with the ladies.
She reads *Anne of Green Gables* to her sons,
protests the global gag rule, revises
her YA novel. On her daughter's birthday,
she requests donations for rescue puppies.
She stocks her fridge with lox, brie,
and half-and-half for her grown children,
when they visit. Last night, she slept fitfully
(stayed up too late watching *Hidden Figures*).
She never was a whiz at math but admires
those who are. This morning, she's weary
and could use help saving the barrier reefs.

BLOOD, RAIN

No more games of dress-up
pretending to be twins
in hand-me-downs from cousins oceans away.

No more endless afternoons with dolls
who shone like ten-franc coins.

God, hold the worlds we made for them,
worlds within worlds. The question
with the trick, you asked it first.

Of course I chose the smallest apple
 (you knew I would).

On bikes we doubled-up. No way
not to kill a road frog sometimes. No one knew
of our whereabouts for hours.

It was like that, the field play, the gallivanting.

Still, somewhere in Armor,
two girls build forts of stone, wood, fern,
elude bulls, devise traps to catch their brothers.

Until they return—medalled in mud,
blood, rain—a raft sinks into the pond.

ALEGRÍA
Pour Elodie

Now she crawls up mud piles, down
steps, in sand, over pebbles, or stones,
soft and sharp, through grass, past bones—

deer carcasses the dogs dug up, left
at the edge of the woods for the coyotes
to feast on. Here, watch her ride her bike

upside down on a tightrope in the cosmos
of a thousand concertos. She is one of the stars.
No, she is one of the moons—her trapeze

vanishes into the night. Under her dome,
Olive becomes *agua*, her weathervane
Lab who serves as after-meal vacuum.

I will buy her the sky. If not for sale, every
Eyewitness book on Amazon—*Train, Castle,
Spy, Whale, Wonders of the World, Mummy,*

*Money, Mesopotamia, Human Body, Desert
Electricity*—so she knows life as more
than a pairing up, so she'll spell the self galactic!

"See the networks of nerves inside your head."
"Discover the earth's ... minerals in close-up."

CORDELIANELLA

Lear never was my father: he is
my mother; my heath, Brittany;
my castle, Le Mont St. Michel,
with its tidal sands that swallow
horses, passengers, carriages whole.

The cage of my own silence is almost
too much for me to bear. My marathon
rigor, my teatime distaste for pedestals,
even as I sit on a throne in an alabaster
gown, rubies stuck in my throat.

The price for passage was always
merger, which I refuse to pay,
though I still beg for forgiveness
like a clover puppy already mud-rained
and chanting: *one will shag & one will hang.*

Am I then my dead father's favorite—
middle-aged, in sooty rags—
or her stepsisters, bald cypress trees
who flatter, then gouge out eyes,
who squeeze square feet into shoes

never meant for them? If neither,
allow me then a plump pumpkin,
a few mice to call friends, a hearth
to sweep at dusk, and a someday prince
who'll coax sonatas out of moonshine.

CONSTELLATIONS, DISCARDED

I despair of ever learning
constellations or stick-shift,
memorizing exceptions

to grammar rules.
Instead I remember
the outfit I wear

the last day we see Daddy
in St. Brieux. We walk, you
hold our hands. We eat

burgers, we say our a-
dieus. We move
to America, I was

fourteen: a cashmere
sweater, soft pink; a blue
skirt with flowers, fading—

set aside weeks before
out of everything packed,
or discarded, for you.

THE VALLEY

The wheelchair couple whose house
flooded with every big downpour
refused to move, declined all outside
help. I think of them now and the part of
town where my father lived briefly
in a furnished room where he once served us
a rotisserie chicken with peas and gently
reprimanded me for sitting too close
to the TV. He'd bought us a game I played
maybe twice, a wooden labyrinth
with a silver marble I weaved along
an open tunnel to its final exit.

BEES

Open up your hives, o bees, cyphers on the fringes
of childhood, honeyed inheritance of self
among others.
My grandfather and godfather carved
their pockets of solitude
by donning white suits. Meticulous, industrious natures,
each quietly worshipped a queen,

each quietly stoked my inheritance. How could I
have known the vastness
being stored up for me, how it would remain
long after the bees had flown.
The moment I was handed the comb
dripping, the stickiness, the wax
in my teeth, the overwhelming sweetness.

It's over now. The bees, long gone, belong
to barefoot gardens, deserted.
Summer no longer sleeps
one foot swollen in her ice-bucket. Jars of
honey no longer arrive
from Lyon, broken in the mail.

A LARCHMONT ELEGY

Let me hide my grief somewhere
in a bathroom stall where someone
scrawled *Te Quiero* on a blank
postcard and mailed it to Bob.

I came to life under
a raven's gaze as if seen
for the first time. But Time
ran off like a pepper grinder.

Love threw out the pheasant
we purchased from a country
store, frozen, and in need
of a Chopin recipe.

CATHEDRAL CAFÉ

If you are a World War II bomb
    I am the cathedral in ruins
If you are the people-watching Gauloises
    I am the Café des Deux Magots
If you are the missing communion fork
    I am the silver spoon who remembers
If you are the stainless steel fridge
    I am the expired pickles and the sour milk
If you are the August blackberries
    I am the stain that won't wash off
If you are the paper without a blank
    I am the last crayon in the box
If you are the frozen pond
    I am the duck trapped under the ice
If you are the pine's shadow
    I am the shadow of the poplar's shadow
If you are the map without countries
    I am the city of barricades
If you are the orphan pennies
    I am the fountain of remorse
If you are the jammed mailbox
    I am the postcard who likes to wait
If you are the staples without a stapler
    I am the line without a ruler
If you are the church of hesitations
    I am the cathedral in ruins

THE TROUBLE SOMETIMES WITH LOSING A SOCK

is how it unlocks
all the other losses
unrelated to socks

ARMPITS

I despise pit stains on my white shirts.
They manifest within hours!
What's the point of buying white shirts?
I can still wear my favorite blouses under a cardigan
the way my mother did.

I only use Tom's natural deodorant: fresh apricot
(no aluminum). Easier to pull off
in the summer with sleeveless dresses.

Once I paid the extra bucks for extra-strength
antiperspirant. Of no use! My armpits got drenched
within seconds. I bombed the interview.

When I try to explain the location of the city
where my grandmother lives, I say,
"It's in the armpit of France."
I gesture, then point,
though it's never a flattering metaphor.

Sometimes I catch a whiff of armpits
from a foreign man who doesn't yet know
we don't do armpits in the States,
the way the smell catches my nostrils
uncomfortably, with pleasure;
or the smell of my own armpits when I wake up
in the morning, sweet and sickening.

Sometimes I even let my armpit hair grow stubbly
but never anything that can't be retracted.
Smelly armpits and hairy armpits are VERBOTEN
in this country. They mean, Beyond Caring.

I long for a nation of armpits where women and men
can braid their smelly armpit hairs into crowns.

DREAM DISTORTIONS

1
Soutine refuses to paint seascapes.
The sand and the sea demoralize him.
He locates waves elsewhere: in trees,
in houses, in villagers, in hanging poultry.

2
My mother no longer feeds me
bites of Toblerone in Paris
museums to prevent whining;
to mouth art, pleasure, learning.

3
Maudit Modi befriends Soutine
who quits les Beaux-Arts to haunt
the Louvre instead. Rembrandt
teaches this shtetl boy everything.

4
My mother expresses a sudden
(urgent) preference for Soutine.
She's adamant I learn
about aging before aging.

5
A doctor extracts a bedbug
from Soutine's ear. Neighbors complain
of meat-rotting smells emanating from carcasses
he enlivens with slaughterhouse blood.

6
In the museum store, my mother insists
on buying me the poster of Monet's boathouse.
Soon her own mother will die,
and she'll be diagnosed with breast cancer
and rheumatoid arthritis.

7
*Enter my nightmare, my fairy-tale,
my feverish dream-twist,
before I slash it with a knife.*

8
In the garden in the rain, I apply lip gloss.
"Me too," my mother says.
With our pink lips shining, we forget
Soutine, we vanquish death and rotting.

9
This painter is not cajoled by money,
cares nothing for connections,
dispenses with symbolism,
cakes paint on his canvas.

10
Outside in the garden, it is raining.
Outside in the rain, the mother and daughter are walking.
A light sort of rain, a light sort of rain.

DEAR JIGSAW

puzzles who wait for me unopened
in boxes on toy store shelves, in warehouses,
at the bottom of a closet in a crumpled paper bag—

Dear favorite puzzles in circle shapes with quaint scenes
at the fair, by a frozen pond, in a mountain town, by the seaside,
where animals always know what to do:
a Dalmatian greets guests at the door, a horse pulls a buggy up a hill,
and a cardinal rests on a creek rock.

Even with scenery, you seek to harmonize:
a lamppost reaches the sea to touch an ocean liner,
and no matter the hour, there's always a Ferris wheel that keeps on
spinning and cotton candy you can keep on eating—

Dear second-favorites: the deserted
terrace of a look-alike Montmartre café or the interior
of a wedding gown boutique after closing—

Dear puzzles I'll never buy unless that's all that's left: the license plates
of all fifty states, the unicolor ones, or the map
of Vermont with pinned attractions—

And dear one who looked away: a rush-hour rocking
on elephantine legs in the snow-globe space
of a metro car. You refused me the satisfaction of a piece that fits,
the thrill of two mismatched patterns belonging.

You did not care to indulge my small pleasures,
my not-looking-at-the-box-top discipline.
Just this once, manifest for me like an expressionist
gallery or sponge animals springing from plastic capsules.

All of you! Alleviate my dread of the missing!
Clear the cobwebs from my brain's park trail
so suddenly, plop, I'm back
in the midst of a Saturday afternoon of endless play
for no reward, tracing my mandala in the wet sand.

HORSES

A Sunday feel to the air.
Puffs of cloud mill about a clear sky,
a breeze teases a stream,
and under a canopy of trees, a country
road stretches onward while grass encroaches
as if colored in by a child, and a few fields
away, a boy, pocket-full-of-marbles, rings
a church bell.
                A shadow-show cutout
—part-train, -carriage, -motorcar—
advances. It lacks texture.
This only belies its unrelenting
forward motion, how it allows for no one else
on the road, not even the horses, the wild, wild
horses heaving, panting alongside, manes
of sweat and soot, entangled. Unaware
the vehicle grazes a flank with a spur. A colt bucks up
in pain. Forget the tenderness
in his eyes. Vanish
                blue sky, white clouds
and gurgling stream. No more bell echoes
in the Sunday distance. At recess
the boy loses all his hard-won marbles
to the school braggart. Wind and rain batter
the trees, disrupting the bucolic lines.
Of course the horses will never
reclaim the road.
                In the gardens of Villandry,
a Beethoven symphony booms out
from a scratchy gramophone.
                Where can a cloud hide
in that blue expanse of sky? It's hard
to pinpoint the century, so let's say, sometime
in the future, where the gardens are exactly
as I remember—a feat of manicured imagination—
though no one is left to maintain them, except
for the horses who have also found their way here.

SOCIETY OF FIREFLIES

When it was warm enough, you came with your nighttime
show, costing us nothing. We caught you in Mason
jars, hoping to create a new kind of bedside
lamp. Leave days rationed out by the computer,
hoarded for a vain flicker of freedom. Weekends,
I zone out on *Homeland*. Sordid. I do enough
careful work to satisfy my bosses. I save
for retirement—to my bohemian eyes,
a fortune—though they say you need more
than a million. Immerse yourself in the exponential
power of dividends. And what about decorating
your rental apartment? At least put up some
curtains after fourteen years. I don't mind
the metro, eavesdropping on other people's
lives. I don't die down there every day
a little. And you rise up once more
unsolicited from the fields, with your equal
measure of appearing and disappearing.

NOTES

1. This collection is named after the Parisian hotel where Charlotte Corday wrote her manifesto in 1793.
2. "My Urban Monastery" is an imitation of Derek Walcott's "Tomorrow, Tomorrow" and is dedicated to Barbara Heim.
3. "The Cicada" is my re-imagining of "The Cricket and the Ant," a Jean de la Fontaine fable I memorized as a French schoolgirl.
4. "A Breton Wife" is my attempt at a Breton rendering of "The River-Merchant's Wife: A Letter" by Ezra Pound, After Li Po.
5. "Alegría" is inspired in part by a Cirque du Soleil show of the same name and references titles from the DK Eyewitness nonfiction series for children. The two quotes are from the back covers of *Human Body* and *Rocks & Minerals*.
6. "Cordelianella" is a mash-up of two fictional characters: Cordelia and Cinderella.
7. "Cathedral Café" is an imitation of Octavio Paz's poem "Movimiento."
8. "Café du Monde" is inspired by Louis Moreau Gottschalk's musical compositions.
9. "Bees" is dedicated to two beekeepers, my grandfather Francis Markoe Rivinus and my godfather Jean-Michel Ribault.
10. "A Larchmont Elegy" is a farewell letter to The Larchmont, a New York City hotel that closed its doors.
11. "Feminine Mystique" is dedicated to the girls and women in my life and the world over.
12. "Dream Distortions" is inspired by Chaim Soutine's paintings at the Barnes Foundation and Stanley Meisler's biography *Shocking Paris*.

Maya Ribault is a French-American poet based in Washington, DC. She is a graduate of Georgetown University and the Bennington Writing Seminars where she was a Jane Kenyon Scholarship recipient. In addition, she has found support and inspiration for her poetry through Bread Loaf Writers' Conference, New York State Summer Writers Institute, for which she was awarded a full-tuition scholarship, and a Virginia Center for the Creative Arts residency. Her poetry was shortlisted for the 2017 Faulkner-Wisdom competition. Alongside her publications, her translation of a 19th century French sonnet appeared in *Speak*. She currently works as a book production editor for a nonprofit press.

www.ingramcontent.com/pod-product-compliance
Lightning Source LLC
LaVergne TN
LVHW040116080426
835507LV00041B/1094